Selling Secrets

The experts tell all!

About the author
Nick Constable BA (Hons)
is the founder of Redline
Associates Ltd, a professional
sales training company based in
the UK. He has 24 years of sales
experience, having begun his
career in 1986. Nick has held
senior sales positions for start-
ups, medium-sized companies
and major global organizations
in the technology sector. He has
recruited, trained and led large
sales teams, managed global
clients for Fortune 100
companies, and as Sales
Director, driven growth in the
demanding environment of
quarterly business cycles for
publically listed companies.

Selling
secrets

Collins

A division of HarperCollins*Publishers*
77-85 Fulham Palace Road, London W6 8JB

www.BusinessSecrets.net

First published in Great Britain in 2010 by HarperCollins*Publishers*
Published in Canada by HarperCollins*Canada*. www.harpercollins.ca
Published in Australia by HarperCollins*Australia*. www.harpercollins.com.au
Published in India by HarperCollins*PublishersIndia*. www.harpercollins.co.in

1

A catalogue record for this book is available from the British Library.

ISBN 978-0-00-732808-6

Printed and bound at Clays Ltd, St Ives plc

Contents

The secrets of successful selling

A few years ago, when the world of business was gripped by the Internet boom, it was fashionable to predict an end to traditional selling done by humans. Michael Dell, to name but one, was showing the world how to sell complex technology on a website. The tantalizing prospect of doing away with expensive salespeople was seriously entertained.

But 10 years on, professional selling is just as vital to the conduct of good business as it ever was. And over the 25 years that I have been selling, the skills and techniques have evolved with the development of technology and markets. It's a highly sophisticated profession.

I've been a successful salesperson, a sales manager and a sales director for companies large and small, and I've been able to observe the very best and the worst in sales practices. Selling isn't, as some will tell you, all about instinct. As I've seen when running my training courses, if you learn the techniques and skills that have been proven to work, and then develop the right attitude, you too can be one of the best.

This book will share 50 of the fundamental **secrets** of how to excel in this exciting profession, whilst, I hope, having some fun and building some great relationships with those you meet, along the way. The 50 **secrets** are divided into seven chapters:

■ **How and why people buy.** If you understand the real motivations people have for buying, you're half-way to becoming a smarter salesperson.

■ **Selling to the right people.** Don't waste your valuable time with the wrong people. Learn how to identify the ones who will buy.

■ **Generating new business.** No business can grow without finding and winning new clients. Learning to do this for yourself will make you a 'self-sufficient' salesperson.

■ **Meeting the customer.** Selling is about human interaction and behaviours. The precious time you spend with customers is when those things matter most.

■ **Making your pitch.** Whether you're writing a proposal or delivering your presentation, there's a lot to think about to make your offer compelling.

■ **Gaining commitment.** Reaching a satisfactory agreement, whilst negotiating the obstacles, takes patience and planning.

■ **The right attitude.** Your success will depend on your willingness to develop the personal motivation and desire to win.

You might be completely new to sales, or an old-timer like me, but I am certain that if you follow the tips and techniques in this book you will see the positive effect on your own achievements!

Selling relies on a set of professional skills that will improve with practice and persistence.

How and why people buy

In this first chapter we are going to explore how and why people buy. Even the smallest transactions rely to some extent on the trust and respect between the seller and the buyer. Understanding the motivations people have for investing their money with you is the first step on the road to learning the behaviours and skills that create great business relationships.

1.1

Sell positive change

Let's start not by considering what you need to do to become a great salesperson, or how good your products or services need to be; let's start by thinking about customers, and the real reasons why they might spend their money with you: it's often little to do with the technical excellence of your product, but because they want to change something.

It has always surprised and amused me that there are so many business people out there who think selling is a science, and want to find (or be sold) a mechanical formula which will always work. Actually, although there are indeed proven techniques and methods that you can learn, selling is much more of an art – it's about behaviours, emotions, communication and people.

Buyers are just people like you and me, and if they are to be persuaded or helped to make a purchase from you, they have to feel that the result for them will be some kind of positive change – in their lives, or in their company's life.

Let's look at a simple example, and imagine that you are thinking about buying a new mobile phone. You've seen lots of the latest models in adverts, but they're expensive, and up until now you haven't been in any rush. Your current phone still works OK, so why spend money on a new one? That new phone will have to offer something which will improve your life in some way.

For example, you might want to pick up email on the move and you can't do that today. You're not buying a phone, but the positive change in the way you can communicate. Later, we'll look at how a great salesperson might have helped you to see how important that positive change is to you.

Every successful sale happens because the buyer comes to believe the product or service will make a positive impact.

1.2

Understand value

It's amazing how many people think that selling is just about the product and its price. Offer something with a fancy new feature at an attractive price and it will sell itself. But that's just marketing, not selling. Value is the most important concept in selling.

Let's consider some of the aspects of value in a business context:

■ **Needs.** We can define Needs as being those drivers of positive change that will deliver the most value to the customer, because these are things the customer must have in order to achieve the improvement they seek. If we can understand how much the customer needs that improvement, we can work out the true value of helping them achieve it.

■ **Wants.** Some drivers of positive change will be 'nice to have' but not completely necessary for the customer to achieve the improvement they seek. We can call these things Wants. The customer will attach less value to these things. Make sure you are not selling to Wants alone.

"The wheel that squeaks the loudest is the one that gets the grease" Josh Billings, American humourist

one minute wonder If you're having difficulty trying to work out what's going to be valuable to your target customer, focus on your customer's customer. Find out what your customer needs or wants to improve in order to deliver value to its own customers. This will give you some clues about what change might represent value to them.

■ **Creating value.** As we'll see later, our job as salespeople is to uncover Needs and Wants, and then to understand how important satisfying them will be. Great salespeople know how to connect what they are selling to the impact, or value, it will create.

■ **Problems, pain and opportunity.** It's highly likely that a positive change is needed or wanted because the customer currently has some kind of problem or difficulty. It's helpful to think about these problems as business 'pain' from which the customer seeks some relief. Depending on how painful the problems are, the value of solving them will increase, and our opportunity to provide a solution will develop.

■ **Three types of value.** There are three basic types of value: Financial value is defined in money terms, Personal value relates to the buyer's own personal agenda or interests, and Business value relates to more general or strategic business aims, not necessarily quantifiable in money terms.

The customer needs to see that the value of your product or service outweighs its price.

1.3

Know the selling cycle

Making a sale can be a long and complex process, involving many different activities. Each of these activities belongs to a phase or stage in the 'selling cycle', and it's important to keep track of what stage you are at with each customer.

Although they might not take weeks or even hours, but just minutes, even short, quick sales will still follow this cycle.

1 **Suspects.** These are brand new leads or opportunities which you have identified but not yet contacted. You suspect they may fit your profile of a potential customer.

2 **Prospects.** These are potential customers with which you have made contact, perhaps by telephone, and established a basis for further discussion, because there is a Need or Want. By this stage, you have discovered a problem that you can help them with.

3 **Opportunities.** At this stage you will be working with the customer to uncover the value to them of solving their problems. You will be building your relationship and finding out more about their Needs and Wants.

one minute wonder Don't imagine that just because a potential customer calls you and asks you how much your product or service costs, that you are already miraculously at the Negotiating stage! Often, this is just an expression of mild interest and means you are really only at the Suspect stage with them.

4 **Proposing.** You will have reached the stage with these customers at which you have enough information and a good enough relationship to be able to put forward your proposal: this is the part of the process where you have the chance to tell the customer about your product and why it's the right choice for them.

5 **Negotiating.** Only when the customer has accepted in principle the proposal you have made will they begin to want to agree the terms on which they may buy. This is the Negotiating stage.

6 **Closing.** Closing is the stage of the Selling Cycle at which you seek firm commitment from the customer to buy.

After Closing, the work hasn't finished, because you will need to think about how you can repeat the cycle and find more business with your customer. That second and third sale ought to become easier too, because the customer now knows what you can do for them!

Use the Selling Cycle to identify your progress with potential customers.

1.4

Build trust and respect

One of my first ever customers told me that he had never bought anything from someone he didn't like. I have seen the truth in this many times over. You need to build a customer's trust and respect.

The way you treat your customer will tell them whether you're someone they want to do business with. Here are five important things to consider throughout the selling process:

■ **We buy from people we like.** You sometimes have to make an effort to get onto the same wavelength as your customer and try to create some rapport. It doesn't mean caving in to their every demand, but developing your ability to be sensitive to their personality.

case study Recently, I was discussing sales training with a sales manager at a large software company. I told her honestly that sending all her people on a training course might not be the best way of improving sales results. In fact, I went further, and told her I did not think training courses on their own

> "When dealing with people, remember you are not dealing with creatures of logic, but creatures of emotion"

Dale Carnegie, author of 'How to Win Friends and Influence People'

■ **Take an interest.** The quickest way to build rapport is to stop talking about yourself, and start showing some genuine interest in the other person's work, problems and personal interests. This is sometimes called 'empathy'.

■ **Do something surprising.** Find something to say or do that will break through the natural cynicism they may have for salespeople, and show them you are different.

■ **Be a 'capable friend'.** You will often find opportunities to bring something extra to the table, such as information, your expert advice or superior knowledge. Your customer will start to see more value in working with you.

■ **Know when to trade.** You won't gain respect if you just do everything the customer demands. When you're asked for something they value, ask for something reasonable in exchange.

Be open, honest and interested in your customer to build their trust.

always worked. It's the opposite of what she expected me to say, but I had started to build her trust in me with a bit of honesty. Of course, this had the benefit of allowing me to explain why several different training approaches, including coaching, might work better for her team.

1.5

You are the difference

One of the most powerful ways of winning against the competition is through the relationship that you build with your customers. You, and the approach you take, make the difference.

A good example of this is the way in which we all choose between suppliers of very similar commodities. There might be four hairdressers in the town where I live, but I always go back to the same one, because I enjoy the company of the chap who cuts my hair, even though he is a little more expensive than the others.

■ **You are unique.** Remember that your relationship with the customer is the one thing that the competition cannot copy. In a close, competitive contest, your behaviour and approach will make the difference.

> **case study** Ian's sales manager was unhappy that Ian wasn't visiting the customers more regularly. Ian thought he could be more efficient just telephoning and sending letters. His boss didn't see it like that. "I might as well send out a catalogue, instead of employing expensive salespeople!" he told Ian.

"To give real service you must add something which cannot be bought or measured with money, and that is sincerity and integrity**"** **Douglas Adams, English comic writer**

■ **Be visible.** It goes without saying that if you're not making the effort to stay in regular touch with your customers and prospects, you can quickly become invisible, and perhaps the representative of another company gets the chance to exert their influence instead. This is sometimes called 'mind-share'. Find reasons to call, to visit, and keep yourself at the forefront of the customer's mind.

■ **Push and pull.** The key to maintaining a winning relationship that makes the difference in a sale is to achieve the right balance between 'pushing' and 'pulling'. Pushing means keeping yourself visible without annoying or irritating the customer with your constant 'nagging'. Pulling means drawing the customer into the relationship using 'Business Doctor' skills (see 4.7), for example, showing empathy, being curious, and adding value by being their 'capable friend'.

A relationship is based on two parties making an investment in it.

The point of employing Ian as one of the company's salespeople was that he could build strong relationships and add value to the selling process through person-to-person communication. He could influence the customer's decision process and build trust for the longer term.

Selling to the right people

One of the most common mistakes made by salespeople, even those with years of experience, is trying to sell to the wrong people. In this chapter we'll look at the importance of identifying the individuals who have the power to make change happen, and the value of analysing the customer's organization to discover the roles that people play in the buying and selling process.

2.1

Understand your customer

Because we salespeople are often under pressure to find new prospects and constantly add more opportunities to the pipeline, we can often find ourselves tempted to chase every possible sales lead. But not everyone who expresses interest actually has the authority, motivation and ability to buy.

Let's look at some pitfalls and how to avoid them:

■ **Who owns the problem?** One of the best guides for identifying the correct people, or person, is to find out who has ultimate responsibility for the business problem or 'pain' that you think you can solve. Remember that they may still lack the authority alone, but it's a good starting point.

■ **Come out of your comfort zone.** It's easy to get stuck in your comfort zone, convincing yourself that those friendly individuals who always take your call are the ones who will buy. This is especially true with existing customers. Force yourself to ask hard questions of yourself and them, and to make new contacts with greater authority.

> **"There are one hundred and ninety-nine ways to get beat, but only one way to win; get there first"**

Willie Shoemaker, American jockey

■ **Make a straw man.** Draw up a profile of your ideal customer, and their attributes, as a sort of test. This is called a 'straw man'. Look at your previous and existing customers. Consider the ideal types of business they are in, and typical job roles.

■ **Spot the 'tyre kickers'.** There's a big difference between people who take great interest in your product, and those who actually have the authority to buy. Some people, and companies, just want a free education, and will give the impression they can buy so that you'll let them play with your product.

■ **Are you first?** Ask yourself: is this customer already evaluating other suppliers? Have you come to the party late? If you're second or third, it might be an indication of their serious intent. On the other hand, experience shows us that if you didn't get there first, you're probably just 'cannon fodder', there to provide a comparative offer.

Do some analysis and research to make sure you target the right companies and individuals.

2.2

Understand their organization

Whether you are approaching a new prospect for the first time, or selling to an existing customer, it's vital to understand how their organization is structured, and who does what. Doing this will help you target the right people with the right messages.

■ **Broaden your horizons.** Your likely starting point with a new customer is often a single person. Find out who else works alongside them, above them and below them. The more contacts you create across the wider organization, the more chances you will have to discover 'pain' and determine how and if they will buy.

■ **Draw the organization chart.** As soon as you can, you should try to draw out the whole of the customer's organization on a sheet of paper, showing the different departments, divisions, teams, individual job titles

case study Alison represented a large software company as the account manager for British Telecom (BT), an enormous UK company. She made it her business to try to talk to every part of their organization, and make contacts at many levels of their hierarchy. It took some time, but eventually she

"If you think you're too small to have an impact, try going to bed with a mosquito in the room"

Dame Anita Roddick, Founder, The Body Shop

and people's names. This is a great way of discovering what you don't yet know, and encouraging you to go and find out!

■ **Identify spheres of influence.** The organization chart will only tell you the official version of the customer's hierarchy. The next step is to take an interest in the unofficial ways in which people within organizations group together in loose 'spheres of influence'. Whose opinions command respect? Who do the senior people listen to? You can map out these connections as you learn more about the people involved.

■ **Pick up clues about the culture.** Of course, every organization is different; not only in the way they are structured, but also in the working culture they have developed. It's important to pick up clues about the way things get done, and observe the accepted norms of behaviour. For example, how much authority is delegated to managers? Is it a sales-led or an engineering-led organization? Is everything done by committee?

Find out how decisions are made at your target customer's organization.

had formed a pretty good picture of how these different teams and departments influenced each other and even competed against each other. One day, a BT director told Alison he always enjoyed speaking to her, because she knew more about how their company worked than he did!

2.3

Know the roles that buyers play

Once you have a clear idea of how your customer's organization is structured, you'll hopefully have the names and job titles of a number of people you want to deal with. The customer may also introduce new contacts to you, as you move through the Selling Cycle. All these people will have a greater or lesser importance to you depending on the role they play.

Let's look at some of these buying roles.

■ **User.** This describes anyone who is simply the intended user of your product or service. Think of them as the ultimate 'end customer' within the organization. Don't overlook them – they have very valuable infor-

one minute wonder List all your contacts and allocate one or more buyer roles to each of them. This will help you to assess how you approach them, how useful they will be, and therefore, how much time and effort you expend working with them.

mation to give you about how your product or service might benefit their organization.

■ **Influencer.** Anyone whose opinion is respected, and who has particular knowledge or interest in your product, can be an influencer of a buying decision. Often, more senior people who make the ultimate decision will rely heavily on people they trust to advise them.

■ **Coach.** The term Coach is used to describe someone who, for whatever reason, wants to help you win the business. They may particularly like your company or product, or dislike the alternatives; perhaps they believe that supporting you is the best way to influence the decision. They are a mine of information if you treat them right!

■ **Blocker.** The opposite of a Coach, these people will either be positively obstructive, or just never do or say anything useful to help you, perhaps because they are afraid of change, or have some other personal reason not to want you to succeed. They will waste your time, so try to spot them early on!

■ **Technical decision maker.** This describes someone with the responsibility of making the product decision first and foremost. Usually, they are middle managers, tasked with evaluating and deciding which technical solution is right for them

■ **Business decision maker.** Usually the owner of the business problem or 'pain', this person is likely to be a senior manager responsible for the business function(s) that will benefit from your product or service.

■ **Financial decision maker.** Usually the Finance Director, this person controls the final decision about whether the money can be spent.

Identify the buying roles of people in a target organization.

2.4

Identify the agents of change

Despite what many salespeople think, it is not always the person with the most senior job title, the biggest office or the largest department who holds true authority in a buying decision. In fact, it may be a mistake to rely solely on people's job titles as a guide to who wields the authority to buy.

■ **Introducing the Agent of Change.** The most important type of all buying roles is someone I'm going to call an Agent of Change. These are often unique individuals within their organization who can make things happen because they not only have enough seniority (which we can identify from their job title), but also possess the personality, drive, insight and motivation to achieve that positive change or improvement in their business.

■ **The natural leaders.** Agents of Change have certain personality traits that give them this unique role. In particular, they are people who are prepared to take a calculated risk and have the personal influence to carry their agenda through. You could call them natural leaders, who do not get bogged down in too much detail, but look at the bigger, strategic picture, and are willing to make bold decisions which create change.

> **one minute wonder** Draw a simple graph with X and Y axes. One axis represents the propensity to take risks and create change. The other represents the level of official authority. Now plot your buyers on this graph. Those in the top right hand corner will be most likely to be agents of change.

■ **Why are they so important?** Because you can't sell to someone who won't change, can't buy and doesn't have a vision of the potential value of improving their business. And we can help give them that vision, as it relates to our product or service!

■ **Sometimes known as Foxes.** Jim Holden of the Holden Corporation, an international sales training company, calls these strange creatures 'Foxes'. They can sometimes be disruptive, demanding and quick to make judgements, but they have the advantage of being highly likely to actually do something positive.

Unfortunately, the vast majority of people we deal with in business are followers – content to let others take the risky decisions. Selling is about convincing someone to do something different, and it can be hard going if we only ever deal with people who want an easy life, or require proof that every decision they make carries no risk.

Look for the rare individuals who combine authority with a willingness to change.

2.5

Get access to authority

It's one thing to have understood the customer's organization and identified all their buying roles; it's another actually to form a business relationship with the decision makers, or the Agents of Change.

Ideally, it should be our goal always to seek access to those with the authority to make buying decisions, even though we will also need to form relationships with people in other buyer roles who will influence them. Here are some things to consider in relation to gaining access to those in authority:

■ **Aiming high.** It's far better to make initial contacts at the most senior level possible, and be referred down to others, than to try to reach authority later by relying on other less senior people to refer you upwards. This isn't always possible, of course. But as a rule, always try to call the most senior person available first.

■ **Delegation.** Even if you only get the chance to have a short conversation with the decision maker, and they refer you downwards, they have effectively 'delegated' the job of dealing with you, and you have now acquired their authority to move forward!

one minute wonder The next time a prospect asks you to travel a long way to a meeting, make a point of asking for the decision maker to be available when you are there. Explain that you will be gathering information about their business problems, and you want to hear the decision maker's perspective first-hand.

■ **Escalation.** If you're only dealing with influencers, they will at some point need to 'sell' to their superiors. Suggest how you can help them – by asking their permission to make contact directly with the decision maker.

■ **Keeping the decision maker informed.** Even if you have never met the decision maker, if they 'own the business problem', you can, with justification, call or email them to keep them informed of what you are doing and how it will benefit them. Do this as early as possible in the process, and keep doing it at regular intervals.

■ **Bargaining for access.** There will be opportunities during a sales process to negotiate for an introduction to a decision maker. If your buyer asks you to do something for them, can you ask to meet a more senior person in exchange?

■ **Dealing with blockers.** If someone is actively blocking your progress towards authority, try going sideways instead. Build alternative relationships and these may open up new paths to the decision makers. Weigh up the risk of going over their heads to the top: annoying them may be less of a problem than losing the whole selling opportunity.

Make every effort to network your way upwards.

Generating
new business

You need a range of techniques and skills to find new opportunities in your chosen markets. If you work for a large organization, it can be easy to rely on the Marketing department to generate leads or just to stay in your comfort zone and try to win all your business from existing customers. But I have found that it is best to become self-sufficient in the art of creating opportunities for yourself.

3.1

Pick the right prospects

The first thing you need to do is decide exactly what sort of customer you are targeting. Here are the five key questions to ask yourself when defining who your target customers will be.

1 **Where are they?** Make it easy for your customers to find you, in the real world or online, and target customers that you can reach with minimum time and effort.

2 **How many of them are there?** It's important to give yourself as many opportunities as possible, so consider how big the total addressable market for your product or service will be.

case study A remark is attributed to Thomas J. Watson, the first CEO of IBM in the early 1950s: "There may be a world market for about five computers." Despite this lowly prediction, IBM continuously

3 **Can they buy?** It's no good going after customers who cannot afford your product or service, or targeting individuals who have no say in the decision. For example, kidney dialysis machines won't be of much interest to a rural doctor, but perhaps his superiors at the main hospital will be in a better position to buy.

4 **Have they heard of you?** If you can identify customers and markets that are familiar with your company or you as an individual, the chances are you'll find contacting them much easier. Also consider if they might know any of your existing customers – if you've already sold to one of their competitors, they could be an obvious target.

5 **Will they change?** No one will buy what you're selling if they don't see a reason to change, do something differently or try something new.

Decide where to focus your research.

targeted its selling efforts at people whom it identified could use its products. Its total address-able market has turned out to be a lot bigger than five computers!

3.2

Make a prospect list

Now you have a clear idea of whom you are targeting, the next task is to start building a list of likely suspects and prospects, and getting yourself organized with a simple system to record your progress. You probably have a few existing customers whom you would like to revisit. But you need to add to this list with lots of new names and contacts.

■ **Get organized.** It might sound obvious, but it is vital that you use a system of some kind to record and organize all your activities. You could use a simple spreadsheet structure in Microsoft Excel, or perhaps you have access to a contact management or CRM system. Even just pen and paper works. Record all the company and individual contact details, and crucially, the next actions for each prospect.

■ **Sources for research.** In the old days, we relied on business directories, and even visits to the local library! Nowadays, the Internet holds a wealth of information about companies and people. Marketing and publishing companies sell this information, and failing that, a bit of desk research using the web and telephone should produce plenty of suspects.

> "It is only the farmer who faithfully plants seeds in the Spring who reaps a harvest in the Autumn"

BC Forbes, founder of Forbes Magazine

■ **Getting the names.** If all you have initially is a company name, getting the names of individual buyers is the next step. Try simply phoning their switchboard and asking for the right person – it often works! Alternatively, find the name of anyone who works there, for example, on the Customer Service desk, and call them, asking for their assistance in contacting the right people. The good news is that most company websites contain the names of senior directors somewhere – try reading through their press releases, for example.

■ **Referrals.** It's amazing how many salespeople overlook the smartest way of gathering new names. Ask your existing customers: "If you were doing my job tomorrow, who would be the first person you'd call?" Explain you are on a drive to generate some new contacts and ask for their help. Remember, though, that you need to have earned the right to seek their help in this way.

■ **Segment your list.** As you build up your list and move through the selling cycle, keep the list segmented into the six stages of the selling cycle (see 1.3).

Gather all your sales leads and research into one place. This is called your 'sales pipeline'.

3.3

Plan your sales campaign

It is good policy to create a plan for your sales campaign. This will help you to think about how you will go about using your limited time and resources to achieve the best results.

■ **Set a goal.** What will success look like? Identify a measurable objective for your campaign, perhaps expressed as the numbers of opportunities in your pipeline, or as a total potential sales value of your pipeline.

■ **Pick a single proposition.** You might have many different products or services you can sell, but don't try to plan a campaign for all of them at once. A better strategy is to pick a single 'value proposition' and focus your energies around this. It's less confusing for the customer too.

"The men who have succeeded are men who have chosen one line and stuck to it"

Andrew Carnegie, Scottish-born American industrialist

Every customer or market is different, so you should think about customizing your approach, using a suitable combination of the following methods of making initial contact.

1   **Email.** A personalized email to a named individual can be a great way of creating initial interest. Don't expect the prospect to respond, though. Emails are easy to ignore, so follow them up with a phone call.

2   **Telephone.** Ultimately, you need to speak directly to your prospect, and if they haven't phoned you, you will need to pick up that phone and make those calls! We'll look at this activity in the pages that follow.

3   **Letters and mailers.** As part of a campaign using other methods, consider the impact of a personalized letter sent in the post. Perhaps you have some relevant company literature that you can use as a reason for writing to the prospect. Try sending letters like this to a number of people at once, including the senior decision makers. This could give you the excuse you need to call them!

4   **Events.** In your market, are there industry events and exhibitions where your prospects gather? Get along there and meet them face to face!

5   **In person.** In some markets, it is acceptable and necessary to call in person at the prospects' business premises. This is a great way of establishing contact.

Work out your methods of approach.

3.4

Play the numbers game

It makes no difference if you are selling ocean liners at $100 million each or selling packets of washing powder, the law of raw numbers is fundamental to sales success. In simple terms, you need to give yourself every chance of winning by getting yourself on the starting grid for as many races as possible.

■ **Activity and effectiveness.** Essentially, playing the 'numbers game' means paying attention to these two pillars of sales success. Activity is the amount of work you put in; effectiveness is the skill with which you execute your plans.

If you work hard and call up a thousand people every month, but have no idea who you are calling or how to speak to them, you're likely to fail. Equally, you might be the best telephone seller in the world, but

"The harder I work, the luckier I get" **Samuel Goldwyn, film producer**

if you only speak to two people every week, you will also fail. So selling, particularly generating new business, is not just a 'war of attrition', it is also a war to be fought using intelligence and skill.

■ **The funnel.** Think about your sales pipeline as a huge funnel. The top of the funnel is very wide, and you can fill it with a great many new suspects. As you move each opportunity through the selling cycle, the numbers of opportunities normally become fewer. At each stage, opportunities will fall away, for all sorts of reasons, some of which will be beyond your control. You can do the maths and work out what your conversion rate is for each stage of the selling cycle. Your conversion rate is affected by your abilities at each stage – your effectiveness.

For example, you might find you are an absolute genius at making new appointments with prospects over the telephone. But for some reason, a lot of these meetings never seem to turn into real opportunities. Your conversion rate at the meeting stage needs some attention! In this way, analysing your raw numbers and your conversion rates will help you to spot bottlenecks in your sales pipeline.

Create a deep pipeline with lots of new opportunities at the top of the funnel.

Selling **secrets**

3.5

Try telephone prospecting

Despite the emergence of Internet advertising, networking events and email marketing, the combined experience of successful salespeople tells us that picking up the telephone and making what are traditionally called 'cold calls' remains the best way of quickly creating new opportunities.

One of the reasons telephone prospecting is so effective is that it will put you in first place every time you open up a new opportunity. Leads that come from adverts or other marketing campaigns are nice to have, but consider the fact that if the prospect has responded to your company, he has also probably signalled his interest to your competitors! That's not good.

case study Recently, I met a salesperson booked onto one of my training workshops, who told me he was already pretty successful, and delighted in informing me he had no need to learn how to cold call. "I get my leads from Marketing and follow every

Getting there first is a golden rule of sales success. It allows you to control the process of uncovering 'pain', creating the vision of value and monopolizing 'mind-share' with the customer. Here are some other golden rules:

■ Don't sell the product. The point of making these phone calls is not to try to make a sale right there and then. The point is to get through the door and get a meeting, so you can use all your interpersonal sales skills to start building a great selling relationship.

■ Be resilient. The truth is that you will inevitably face some degree of rejection and failure during this process. You just have to learn to accept that fact: you can't 'win them all' and you can't expect to. Try to develop resilience, and keep on trying!

■ Don't be obstinate. If you're really getting nowhere, take a deep breath and consider the possibility that your approach is wrong. Don't just blame the customer or the market - change something, and better still, ask the last prospect you called to tell you what they didn't like about your approach.

■ Do it all the time. Because telephone prospecting can be hard work, we tend to do it in fits and bursts. This can lead to 'feast and famine' or peaks and troughs in your pipeline. Do it regularly and keep that funnel topped up!

Phoning people to create new opportunities is cheap, fast and direct.

one of them up," he told me. So I asked him if he was happy with the money he was making. Of course, he said, "No, I'd love to earn more." Taking control of his own success, by learning to use the telephone effectively, was a better solution.

3.6

Create your
60-second pitch

Assuming that you get to speak to the right person, you will have about 30-60 seconds to convince that person to spend more time with you. There are some essential elements in a winning 60-second pitch. You can use the word SHREK – the name of the happy green ogre in the films – to remember them:

■ **S = Say who you are.** Simply introduce yourself politely, and say the name of the company that you're calling from.
■ **H = Hook.** Any connection, personal or company-specific, that you can find to make this a 'warm' call rather than 'cold', is called a Hook. A referral, the name of someone else in their company you have spoken

case study When I was a sales director, I was bombarded with cold calls from recruitment agencies. Most of these people just asked me if I was hiring any people at that time. Generally, I would tell them no, and get them off the phone. On rare occasions, the caller knew how to structure their call. For example:

to or who once worked there, or a relevant fact about them, will work. If your company has a well-known brand name in the market, maybe that's all you need. This is easier if you are targeting an existing customer, but new prospects might require some investigative work.

■ **R = Reason statement.** This is your one chance to put something on their radar that will strike a chord with them. This is a brief sentence explaining what you do, followed immediately by an example of work you have done for similar companies or better still, their competitors. Don't just start telling them how great your product is. Make it specific or relevant, using the opening "…and the reason I'm calling is that…"

■ **E = Effect.** This is a specific fact or example relating to the value or business benefit that you have been able to deliver to other customers, for example: "…and we've been able to help them increase sales last year by 10%." You don't have to have hard numbers here, just try to provide some evidence of the positive impact you could bring to their business.

■ **K = Key question.** Now try to ask a direct question: "Is this something that you might be interested in exploring further? Could we find 30 minutes of your time to discuss this?"

The overall aim of the call is to ask for the opportunity to meet them or get their commitment to a follow-up action.

Develop a pitch using SHREK.

"Hello, I'm Fred, calling from Superman Recruitment. I noticed from your website that you've started offering a solution to the insurance sector, and the reason I'm calling is that we've recently placed a number of salespeople with success in that sector. I was wondering if we could discuss…"

3.7

Develop your telephone tactics

Now you have a compelling 60-second pitch, consider some of the other tactics you will need to employ to deal with the barriers that will inevitably be thrown up in your path.

Selling to organizations usually means having to deal with a variety of obstructive systems, procedures and policies, not to mention staff who are actually paid to stop you talking to their colleagues! However, if you are selling to small businesses or individuals, the job of getting the right person on the phone can be a lot easier.

■ **When to call.** The two most common difficulties you will face are access and availability. When will the person you are targeting most likely be at their desk? How can you get past the inevitable 'gatekeepers' who guard the entrance to their lair? Often the answer is to pick a time of day, and a day of the week, when they are likely to be in the office, but their gatekeeper is not. Early on Monday morning, later in the evening after normal business hours, Friday afternoons, and lunchtimes will all give you an edge. In your culture, there may be other times to consider too.

one minute wonder Most people in business really do like to be helpful, if they can. Appeal to their better nature, by asking politely, "I wonder if you can help me…." Even receptionists told to enforce a 'no names policy', will often respond to a bit of charm, and helpfully offer some suggestions on how to circumvent their own policy!

■ **Direct and mobile numbers.** Far better than wrestling with Reception, obstructive colleagues and secretaries, is the use of a direct or mobile phone number if you can discover it. Sometimes, simply calling someone else in their department and asking them is all it takes.

■ **Getting past reception.** "What's the call regarding?" asks the receptionist. Or "We don't accept sales calls". Who said anything about sales? Just reply that you are simply making an enquiry, doing some research, establishing initial contact on a recommendation, or use your Hook to explain that your call is 'warm' not 'cold'.

■ **PAs and secretaries.** Don't make the mistake of treating PAs and secretaries as an irritation to be avoided or ignored. Make them your friend, be polite and respectful, ask for their guidance and see if they will schedule a time in the diary for you to call and speak to their boss.

■ **Voicemail.** The first time you call and hear a voicemail greeting, inviting you to leave a message – leave a message! This is your chance to leave a succinct 'advert' using a version of your 60-second pitch. Don't try to sell, just explain the reason for your call, and that you will be calling back. Do this no more than four times, before resorting to a different tactic, such as an introductory email.

There's nearly always a different way in, other than through the front door!

3.8

Overcome your reluctance

Even if you have mastered the techniques of telephone prospecting, perhaps the biggest challenge you'll face is actually doing it, and making it a regular activity. It can be disheartening, difficult work. Just getting started is often the crucial hurdle.

This is a mental challenge, and it has to do with overcoming your natural fear of failure and rejection. Consequently, even seasoned sales professionals will often find any excuse to avoid this activity. Therefore, you'll gain a huge competitive edge if you develop mental strength and defeat your fears.

one minute wonder If you believe in your product or service, a great technique for motivating yourself is to remember all the other happy customers you have, and then tell yourself that there will be hundreds of similar organizations just waiting for your call. The next person you speak to could be the one that says, "Thank goodness you called me!"

"There's nothing like a dream to create the future"

Victor Hugo, French Romantic writer

■ **Analyse your fears.** The first step towards achieving this is to analyse what it is that you fear about picking up the phone to make 'cold calls'. It is likely to be either the worry that you will face continuous rejection, or that you will lack the confidence to be convincing when talking to complete strangers.

■ **Face your fears.** You will disprove both of these worries through the act of doing it – that is, facing your fears head-on. That takes courage, and the motivation you'll need will come from having a clear view of what success will mean to you. Create a vision of your success, and think about how you will feel if you can do it. The key here is to get from a frame of mind that says, "I have to do this" to one that says, "I want to do this."

■ **Set realistic goals.** Why do you want to do this? If you spend a whole day telephone prospecting, and you can make three new appointments, how good will that make you feel? Set some realistic goals that represent genuine progress for you in your sales campaigns, and keep reminding yourself of the satisfaction you'll feel when you achieve them.

As well as focusing on a vision of your success, try to recall past successes. If you've seen it work before, you know it can work again, and the more you do it, the better you will get! Your self-belief will develop through practice and preparation.

Don't worry about the "Nos" because a "Yes" is just around the corner.

3.9

Handle objections

No matter how well-crafted your 60-second pitch is, you will inevitably encounter objections. Often, objections are little more than excuses not to do anything right then. Making a decision to say "No" to you is a lot easier than saying "Yes", because the prospect fears a "Yes" means more work for them, even if they like the sound of your offering!

Don't just cave in! Get past the one or two objections they raise to try to put you off, and you will find the opportunity will start to develop. Let's look at some typical objections.

■ **"I'm too busy..."** This is just a brush-off and not a serious objection. Try asking when would be a better time to arrange to speak. Maybe your offering can save them time in any case: "That's exactly why I'm phoning…"

■ **"Send me some literature..."** This sounds quite positive on the face of it, but it is likely to result in your literature ending up in the bin. Explain that you could send literature, but you really don't know what's relevant to them at this stage. Now ask for that meeting to come and discover more about their problems and which of your solutions may be relevant. If nothing else, seek a commitment that they will read the material you send and arrange a time to call back to discuss it.

■ **"It's not my responsibility..."** The prospect is saying they are not the right person to make the decision. Ask who is, and get another name. Now you have a referral to give you the Hook, when you call their colleague.

■ **"We're happy, thank you..."** Ask them to explain what they are already doing. Explain that many of your other customers also do the same, but you've been able to complement it. Nothing is ever perfect, no one is ever completely happy. Try asking: "If money were no object, what else would you improve?" Suggest a brief meeting to enable you to show them the additional improvements you could bring.

■ **"Company policy..."** Again, this is an excuse to do nothing - company policy makes it impossible to change. Ask who makes that policy, get a name or a department. If they already have a contract with another supplier, ask when that contract is due for review or renewal.

Most objections are just forms of hesitation. Move the conversation onto more positive ground.

3.10

Keep yourself motivated

Success comes from dedication to the various tasks we've looked at in this chapter. But keeping yourself motivated is easier said than done. Even if you have a manager applying pressure to perform, the best motivation comes from self-management.

■ **Set realistic goals and a reward.** Give yourself the feeling of real progress by setting small, achievable goals – perhaps for today or this week. As you get better and your results improve, you can stretch yourself. Maybe the reward is simply the result you're aiming for, or perhaps your company will offer an incentive you desire.

case study Jack Welch, the CEO of GE for many years, has said that the single most important thing he always did to keep himself motivated was to write down a list at the end of each day of the actions he would take tomorrow. The following day he would cross these actions off his list as he completed them, and finish each day by writing out

■ Keep a visible record. This might be your prospect list itself. Some sales teams use a white-board on the office wall to record activity and success – and this will introduce a degree of competition which in itself can be motivational. A system of 'traffic light' colours to highlight prospects that have reached certain stages in the Selling Cycle will give you a graphic way of monitoring your conversion rates.

■ Vary the workload. Try to use a mixture of different prospecting approaches throughout the week so that you don't get stuck in a rut. Write some letters to key prospects, go to a networking event, do some desk research and make some calls. Record every small step or break-through and review how you did at the end of the week.

■ Block out time. Give yourself some discipline by scheduling specific times to do certain tasks. Look at your whole week's schedule and make sure you're doing something positive at each stage of the Selling Cycle.

■ Improve your environment. If you're in a noisy office, this can be distracting, so try finding a quiet room in which you can focus on a particular task, such as telephone prospecting.

■ Jump straight back up. If your last call ended in a definite rejection, pick up the phone immediately and dial the next number!

Find visible ways of scoring your successes to build your self-confidence.

his next day's list. This works because it gives a personal sense of achievement, and focuses the mind on getting things done, not just planning to do them. Welch said it also helped to relieve the stress of worrying overnight about all his duties. He is famous for saying: "Control your own destiny or someone else will."

Meeting the customer

What is the difference between marketing and selling? Well, in most cases, marketing is a one-way form of communication that relies on giving information in a way that should appeal to the potential customer. The moment communication becomes two-way – between two people – is the moment it becomes selling. Here we look at how we can make a success of those precious, face-to-face opportunities.

4.1

Plan your sales visit

You'll have probably worked hard to give yourself the chance of a meeting with your new prospect. You will probably only have a short time to spend with them, and what you do or say will affect the outcome of the whole sale. Therefore it is vital that you make the very best of this opportunity.

As with most things in life, a little planning can make all the difference. Here are four essential things to remember:

1 **Set a goal.** What will constitute a successful meeting for you? What is reasonably achievable within the time you have with this prospect? Is it the conclusion of the sale right then or the commitment from the prospect to another meeting, or to receive a proposal from you? Preparing a sensible goal will ensure that you stay on track and allow you to assess the outcome.

2 **Send a brief agenda.** Before the meeting takes place, send a bullet-point summary of the points you want to cover. This will set the prospect's expectations and allow you to control the content of the meeting. It will also allow them to respond if they think you have missed anything important to them.

one minute wonder Plan whom and what you think it is appropriate to take with you to the meeting. Remember that the first stages of a Selling Cycle are about diagnosing business problems and listening to the customer. So perhaps you shouldn't be taking your PowerPoint presentation or stacks of literature along at this stage.

3 **Do your homework.** It's important that you demonstrate to the prospect that you have some understanding of their business and can ask intelligent questions that are relevant. Make sure you do some basic research, perhaps by looking at their website or considering some of the challenges businesses like theirs are experiencing.

4 **Prepare some questions.** Later in this chapter, we'll look at questioning in detail. It is very useful to take into the meeting with you a brief 'questioning plan' or a simple list of the sort of questions you want to ask. This serves as a reminder to you, and helps you to get to your objective.

Time spent with a prospect is precious selling time, so plan carefully for it.

4.2

Make a great first impression

Although a cliché, it is nonetheless true that we humans tend to make very quick judgements about people on first meeting them. Those first few seconds and minutes are crucial, and if you make a bad impression, it can take a lot of work to rectify.

■ **Don't sit down.** If the customer's premises or office has a reception area or foyer where you are expected to wait for them, it's a good idea to remain standing up. Firstly, it's hard for the receptionist to forget about you. Secondly, you are in position to make a more powerful

one minute wonder Try practising your first impressions technique with a colleague or a friend, and ask them to give you some frank feedback about how you come across. You might be surprised by what they say, because none of us are our own best critics. Ask them what they thought about you the first time they met you.

impression when the prospect first claps eyes on you, rather than being slumped in a chair at his or her knee level.

■ **Smile!** A smile can go a long way towards communicating confidence and putting the other person at ease. It's a welcoming gesture that gets everything off on the right note.

■ **Make eye contact.** As the prospect approaches you, make an effort to look directly into their eyes. This is one of the best ways to indicate that you're trustworthy and confident. You'll also be able to tell something about them from their eye contact or lack of it.

■ **Dress smartly.** In Western cultures it is a golden rule that at first meetings you should wear a business suit. Whatever part of the world your meeting is in, make sure you look professional, smart, clean and tidy, without being too ostentatious. No one wants to deal with someone who is signalling poor self-respect or arrogance through their dress sense.

■ **Small talk.** Most meetings start with a bit of small talk or casual conversation. This is a good thing, especially if it 'breaks the ice', but don't let it carry on for more than a couple of minutes. You're there to talk business, not discuss the weather or the traffic!

■ **Which chair?** If you're faced with a choice of places to sit, try not to sit directly opposite. Try to sit next to the prospect, or between them if there is more than one person attending.

■ **Get a business card.** Once you've arrived in the meeting room, start by requesting the person's business card or similar contact details. You can check their job title and reciprocate by offering your card. This is a formality, but is easily forgotten.

Give subliminal messages that you are a trustworthy and credible individual.

4.3

Adapt your style

Human beings are social creatures by nature, and we subconsciously send out all sorts of signals to the other humans we meet by how we act, speak and dress. If you can pick up and exploit these clues, you will have some pretty powerful short cuts towards establishing great relationships.

Not only are great salespeople acute observers of these signals in other people, but they learn to adapt their own style accordingly. Let's be clear about this before we go on: this is not an invitation to become an actor, or to start pretending to be someone you are not. It is, however, about being able to change your behaviour subtly in order to connect more easily at the human and social level, and to establish rapport.

case study Raoul was at a meeting with a number of people all of whom were wearing smart suits and earnestly discussing their project. Raoul hadn't remembered to get everyone's business cards or names. One of these people was dressed very casually, and seemed mainly interested in cracking jokes. So Raoul ignored him, and focused his

■ **Body language.** The key concept here is sometimes called mirroring or style matching. The most obvious example of this is body language. The next time you are able to observe two people together who clearly get along well, you might notice how they subconsciously copy each other's body postures. It's natural human behaviour and we can exploit it. Your prospect leans back in his chair and crosses his legs. A few seconds later, do the same. Don't be too obvious, and don't do it every single time!

■ **Speech.** You can do the same thing with what you say and how you say it. Listen to the other person's style of speech and vocabulary. Are they happy using very casual language and slang? Or are they very precise and technical? How comfortable will they feel if your own language is completely opposite to theirs? Try to pick up their organization's jargon, and use it.

Although generalizations can be dangerous, the clues people give us through their body language, dress and speech are all ways of working out what sort of personalities they are. If, for example, they're analytical introverts with a passion for detail, and you're the opposite, they are unlikely to work with you unless you can adapt your style a little.

Keep your eyes and ears open, and be sensitive to people's moods.

attention on the professionals. Only later did he discover that the scruffy fellow was the CEO of the company. He felt he had earned the right to dress how he pleased, and had the personal confidence to amuse himself during the meeting. The point is that generalizations are a dangerous thing, and you can't make judgements based on style alone!

4.4

Telling isn't selling

Selling is a two-way communication, and the direction of information flow that is most powerful is the one from the prospect to the vendor, not the other way around. If you think that selling is all about doing all the talking about facts and figures yourself, you will not be very effective.

Imagine you are selling a complex technical product. It has a great many clever features and lots of customers love it. Now imagine you've got half an hour with an important new prospect. They're interested in your product, and invite you to tell them about it. What do you do?

The temptation of a great many salespeople is to use that half an hour to try to convey to the customer every aspect of its capabilities, perhaps even to try to demonstrate it to them. You end up talking and talking, trying to get all that great information out of your mouth. But how do you know whether anything you're saying is relevant to the prospect's business or their challenges? You're making assumptions, and you've turned into nothing more than a talking brochure!

one minute wonder The next time a prospect invites you to explain your offering, ask yourself whether you are yet in a position to customize your pitch based on your detailed understanding of their situation. If not, politely decline at this stage, and explain that you would first like to investigate with them which aspects of your offering will be most important to them.

■ **Understand the art of selling.** Remember that you are not there to sell your product. You are there to sell the *value* of what that product might be able to do for the customer – the positive change it can create. So first of all, you must listen and ask questions, even if the customer tells you they want to hear all about the product. Resist the temptation, your chance to do this will come, but later.

■ **Don't just project yourself as 'the expert'.** The other important aspect of selling in this context is the reaction of the prospect to the great deal of unfocused information you are offering: you think you sound like an expert, but experts are usually boring, and it simply comes across as arrogant to assume the prospect wants to listen to every last detail. In addition, what chance are you giving the prospect to respond and engage in a two-way communication with you? You are like a radio on broadcast mode, when you should be more like a telephone!

Wait until you have gathered enough knowledge before making a proposal.

4.5

Questioning is a powerful tool

If we're agreed that telling isn't selling, then what is it that we should be doing instead? The answer is that we should be making every effort to engage the prospect in a dialogue, asking questions and listening to their answers. These two skills are fundamental to the art of successful selling in most business contexts.

Questions are extremely powerful tools which, when used skilfully, immediately create the environment for uncovering business 'pain', discovering needs and wants, and developing a vision of the value you can offer. Let's look at why and how this works.

1 When you stop 'telling', and start asking questions, it has the effect of putting your prospect centre-stage, and giving them a strong feeling that attention is being paid to them. This is flattering, and since most people enjoy talking about themselves, it's a great way of indicating that you have the prospect's best interests at heart.

"Learn from yesterday, live for today, hope for tomorrow. The important thing is not to stop questioning"

Albert Einstein, German-born physicist

2 Questions allow you to listen to what's important to you, without appearing to make assumptions. If in doubt, always ask, rather than tell.

3 Questions are the way to control the dialogue and guide the conversation in the direction you want. That's why politicians are taught to answer a question with another question.

4 Questions make the prospect re-examine their assumptions – about you and about their business. Your careful questioning of their plans, problems and worries could be the first time they have had the chance to think it all through. This is the reason questions are the main tools used in consultative selling.

Remember the two general types of questions: Open questions begin with How, Why, What, Where and When. They elicit information, because you cannot simply answer with a Yes or No. Closed questions can only be answered with Yes or No. They're effective when you want to test an assumption, control the dialogue or qualify an answer.

Try to avoid turning the conversation into an interrogation: you're aiming to demonstrate your genuine curiosity.

4.6

Remember to SPEND!

Let's now look at a very powerful method that uses five different types of question within a simple structure. It's designed to help you gather relevant information, uncover 'pain' and create value. This is a well proven method used by successful consultative salespeople, and it's easy to remember the five questioning steps, as it spells the word SPEND.

■ **S = Situation.** These questions are simply those that gather facts or general information about the prospect's situation, for example, their organization, job roles, current systems, policies and working practices. It's a good place to start when you meet a prospect for the first time.

> **one minute wonder** You might be able to use the whole of this five-step model within the course of a single meeting or phone call. In more complex sales, it may require several meetings, but is essential you complete these steps before you try to propose a solution. Give SPEND a try!

■ **P = Problems.** These questions specifically ask about difficulties, issues, challenges, shortcomings or problems that the prospect may have. They may naturally follow on from a situation question, but must include a 'problem' word like the ones above. You can also ask more positively: "How could that be improved?" This is also a problem question because it gets the prospect to talk about their 'pain'.

■ **E = Effects.** The most important type of question of all, these follow a problem statement by asking what the impact, implication or effect of the problem is for the prospect. By asking about effects, you are beginning the process of uncovering the true cost of the 'pain' and therefore the potential value of doing something about it. Every time the prospect reveals a problem, get into the habit of responding by asking about its effect.

■ **N = Need Agreement.** Once you have discovered the true effects of a problem, you now need to seek agreement that the prospect is willing to do something about it, and believes you can help them. "How do you see us helping with that?" Or: "Is this important enough to fund a solution?" These questions allow you to prioritize which problems have most value if they are resolved. They also allow you to summarize the issues and check that the prospect has a vision for change.

■ **D = Decision.** The final step is to ask for commitment to move forward, based on the agreement of Need. It might be as simple as asking, "How do we move forward?" Or you could suggest the next step, for example, "Can we present our proposal?"

The SPEND questioning model builds a shared vision of value with the prospect.

4.7

Be a business doctor

If you want to show the customer you're different from all your competitors, try acting like a doctor in business: taking time to discuss the customer's circumstances and difficulties will allow you win their confidence and trust. They may open up to you more, and tell you valuable information about why they might want to buy.

Think about what a really good doctor would do when visiting a sick person for the first time:

■ **Don't make assumptions.** Be curious, and try not to think you know what the customer wants. Let them explain their problem and its effects to you.

■ **Listen carefully.** Show the customer that you are listening: this is called 'active listening', for example, keeping eye contact, leaning forwards and responding without interrupting too much. Guide the conversation with your questions.

■ **Diagnose with care.** A great doctor will spend time looking at all your symptoms and even doing tests. You can do the same with your customer, using your questioning skills to uncover the true effect of their problems. We call this finding the 'cost of pain'.

"You will make more friends in a week by getting yourself interested in other people than you can in a year by trying to get other people interested in you"

Arnold Bennett, English novelist

■ **Agree the best result with the customer.** Once you have diagnosed business problems, and their cost, ask permission to propose suitable options and agree with the customer what will work best.

■ **Be honest, build trust.** There are lots of occasions in selling when you are faced with a choice whether to tell a lie or be honest, even if the effect may be negative for you. Generally, being honest is always the best policy: in the end, if you lie about your product or service, your customer will eventually discover this. But if you are open and direct with a customer about a shortcoming, they will instantly know they can trust you, and therefore, your product.

■ **Don't propose too early.** How many times do you find yourself telling the customer how great your product is just after you meet them? It's easy to dive in and offer a solution every time the customer mentions a problem that we think we can solve. But any proposals or offers made when we should still be diagnosing can appear pushy and arrogant.

If a customer's interested, they will respond well if you genuinely help them to make the right decision. Professional selling is not about forcing or tricking people, but helping them to want to buy from you.

Like a doctor treating his patient, try different lines of enquiry before proposing a solution.

4.8

Qualify the opportunity

By now, you've uncovered some business opportunities based on specific problems the customer is willing to spend money on to resolve. The next step is to find out if they really can buy, when they will buy and how that decision will get made.

Unfortunately, there are far too many customers out there who will waste your time: they may want to buy, but can they? Let's look at some vital qualification questions. These are essentially tests of the prospect's commitment to the process and their ability to make a purchase.

1 **Decision makers.** We need to discover who exactly holds the power (or authority) to make a purchasing decision. As we've already seen, this may be several people, it may be a committee, or it may be a single individual, helped by their Influencers. Even when the prospect asserts that they can make the final decision, always ask who else will be involved.

2 **Timescales.** Ask some questions that give you a clear understanding of the time-frame within which the prospect expects to be able to buy. This will give you a better idea of their sense of urgency and may also reveal other obstacles they think they will encounter in the process. It may also allow you to set a deadline for the purchase, perhaps contingent upon a special price.

3 **Budgets.** Have they actually got any money? Can they spend it? Don't make any assumptions: even though a budget may be available in principle, there could be some complex internal constraints in place. Organizations often deliberately make it extremely difficult for their employees to spend anything!

4 **Process.** We need to work out exactly what the internal process is for producing a written commitment to buy, such as a purchase order. Who will do this, and what information will they need? I have seen a great many sales fail at this hurdle because a purchasing function introduces new rules or requirements at the last minute.

A word of warning: if a prospect gives you all the answers to these questions early in the Selling Cycle, it could be an indication that they are already at an advanced stage with another supplier, and you're just there to provide a comparison!

Qualification questions are really just Situation questions helping you to test the level of the buyer's intent.

4.9

Silence is golden

Assuming you're well on your way to becoming a master of asking SPEND questions and qualification questions, you'll be full of things to say to the prospect when you meet. So let's not forget the counter-balance to speaking, which is silence, and the ability to keep your mouth shut.

Most of us in the selling profession love to talk. However, knowing when to be silent is very important.

Imagine you've just asked your prospect a particularly important question. The prospect sits there fiddling with their pen, and doesn't say a word for a few seconds. What's the result? The temptation is all too strong to jump in and fill the silence with the sound of your own voice. If you can resist that temptation, silence has a number of benefits:

case study Charles and his manager visited a charity organization to close a big deal. They met the IT Director, and towards the end of the meeting, Charles asked the vital Decision question: "Have we done enough to earn your business?" There were a few seconds of silence. Because Charles was young and excited at the prospect of winning his first big

■ **Makes the prospect think.** The longer you sit there in silence, the more time it gives for the prospect to think about their answer. The result could be something dramatic.

■ **Forces a response.** Don't let the prospect off the hook, by suggesting the answer for them! Force them to come up with their own answer.

■ **Shows respect.** Especially in Asian cultures, your silence is a signal that you respect the other party and what they are about to say. I once sat in silence for over ten minutes with a Japanese businessman, while he considered his options! It would have been disrespectful had I tried to encourage his thought process with more words from me. I did get the sale (in the end!).

Don't interrupt. Let the prospect tell you the whole story. Often, answers come in more than one stage. There's a preliminary and superficial answer, which can often be followed with supplementary information. If you interrupt half-way through, you'll lose the most interesting part of the information.

Don't let silence make you feel uncomfortable: actually, it is a very powerful sales tool.

sale, he couldn't restrain himself and started telling the prospect about all the reasons he had for saying yes, including a few facts he had previously overlooked. Despite his manager kicking his shins under the table in an attempt to shut him up, he had succeeded in raising a number of new objections on the prospect's behalf. They lost the sale that day!

4.10

Move things forward

We've looked at some important aspects of face-to-face meetings with customers and prospects. But all our efforts will have been wasted if we are unable to develop the relationship we have formed, and move the Selling Cycle on further.

It may be the case that you have done your job so well that the customer needs no more convincing, and has already written out your purchase order. However, in most types of selling, the process involves several more steps, and each one of these represents a very real danger that the sale will grind to a halt.

In my experience, no matter how compelling your proposition, customers have a tendency to drag their feet, lose interest or simply forget what they've agreed to do. This is often because we've just put ourselves onto their 'To Do' list, and we're not a priority.

"The bad news is time flies. The good news is you're the pilot"

Michael Altshuler, American business and sales expert

Here are a few ideas for keeping things moving:

1 **Next actions.** Don't let the meeting finish without agreeing one or two clear next actions, and in particular, at least one action that the prospect will take. It's important not to leave with all the responsibility for further action lying with you. Keep the prospect involved and committed to doing something positive.

2 **Next meeting.** If you possibly can, try to set up a follow-up meeting there and then. This could be to return with a proposal, to meet other parties, especially a more senior member of their team, or to continue your questioning, if you didn't complete your diagnosis.

3 **Write back.** Always remember to write back, or email the attendees at the meeting with a summary of what was discussed, demonstrating your understanding of their specific issues, and recording the next actions you jointly agreed to take. This will serve as an 'audit trail', and will avoid any unpleasant misunderstandings later on.

4 **Involve others.** If you have other contacts at the prospect's organization who did not attend the meeting, write or email to them an equivalent summary of the meeting, keeping them informed of your progress, and asking for their guidance.

Try to agree on the key actions you and your customer need to take next.

Making your pitch

So you have given yourself every chance of learning as much as you can about the prospect's circumstances, their problems and their ability to buy. You have completed your diagnosis and arrived at the point of agreeing a clear vision with the prospect of the value they might attach to the positive change your product or service can bring to their business. It is on this basis that you can now make your pitch.

5.1

Build a business case

Before you're in a position to make your pitch, you should try to assemble all the facts and figures you've derived from your questioning and diagnosis with the prospect, so that you can create a compelling business case, the backbone for your proposal.

This may be something the prospect needs to do anyway, in order to secure funding, and you should try to help them. In any case, it is vital that you relate the proposal to their specific needs and the business value of your offering.

■ **What is a business case?** Your business case is a statement, or explanation, of the value you can offer. Remember the three types of value: Financial, Business and Personal. If you have succeeded in uncovering 'pain', and then the effects, or cost, of that 'pain', you should have the facts and figures you need. Your SPEND questioning is the way to do this.

■ **Get the data.** You may, however, require some additional information. If, for example, you were selling more fuel-efficient diesel vans, you may have discovered that the prospect has a problem currently with their fuel costs, but what is the financial value of moving to your solution? How many miles per year do they drive? What are the average fuel costs per month that they incur today? Get these facts, and you can start to work out the financial value of your new van.

■ **Assess what's measurable.** The above example is fairly obvious, but in many cases, it's more difficult to find relevant data. In these cases, try to work out what exactly could be measured, before and after they have bought your solution. Time, money, space, effort, resources and even personal advancement can all be measured in one way or another. Ask the prospect to help you.

■ **Payback time.** Ultimately, the strength of your business case rests on the measurable value of your solution outweighing its overall price, or cost. This is called its Return on Investment. Can you work out how long it will take? Try to be clear what the pay-back timeframe will be. For example, your customer might have to run those diesel vans for three years before they recoup their investment.

Back up your value proposition with hard facts as well as suggested benefits to create a compelling business case.

5.2

Write a great proposal

The opportunity to prepare and present a written proposal to your prospect is highly valuable as a means of explaining in detail your value proposition, and of giving the prospect some ammunition that he or she can use internally with superiors and other colleagues to drive the decision process.

Here are some tips for structure and content:

■ **Not too long.** There's no real advantage in delivering a massive document that takes hours to read. You need to be succinct, interesting and specific. Avoid just copying reams of product information or marketing literature.

■ **Executive summary.** The first section of the proposal should be the executive summary. This should be no more than one page which summarizes the key benefits and states why yours is the best overall solution. It is so called because it is often assumed this is the only bit that senior people will actually read.

"This report, by its very length, defends itself against the risk of being read" Winston Churchill, British prime minister

■ **Restate the business issues.** The next section should clearly explain your understanding of the prospect's business problems, and why the prospect is interested in doing something about them. This needs to be tailored to the individual customer's requirements.

■ **Propose your solution.** Next, set out how your solution will address these needs. Constantly look for ways to explain how product features relate to solving 'pain'.

■ **Make it FAB!** FAB stands for Feature, Advantage, Benefit, and it's the way to turn a simple fact or feature into a compelling reason to buy. Use the phrase "which means that" to get from a feature to its advantage (why it's better) and finally, its benefit. Here's an example: My mobile phone has a long battery life (Feature), which means that it rarely goes flat when I'm on the road (Advantage), which means that I can stay in touch with customers all the time (Benefit).

■ **State the cost.** At the end of the document, explain your pricing in terms of the business value you'll deliver. Always highlight the savings or return on investment, rather than the price. You might also want to create some urgency by attaching a time limit to your offer.

■ **Deliver it in person.** Whenever possible, ask for a meeting to present the proposal in person. This will allow you to emphasize the strengths and deal with any objections there and then.

Demonstrate that you understand their business needs, and can provide the right solution to address them.

5.3

Present in style!

In many sales scenarios, you will be asked to present your proposal to the person or group of people involved in making the decision. This is a great opportunity, but one which adds some more challenges. A fantastic proposition on paper can be ruined with a poor presentation!

Here are seven important things to remember – and practise:

1 **Standing up.** You'll control the space, be more visible, have better voice projection, and think more clearly on your feet.

2 **Being audible.** Even though nerves can sometimes make you lose confidence, don't mumble or just talk to the person nearest you. Try to project your voice so that everyone can hear you clearly.

3 **Eye contact.** It's very important to give everyone in the room a roughly equal amount of attention, so regularly scan the audience's faces and try to make eye contact with everyone. Don't make the mistake of focusing on just one individual, or staring at your shoes!

one minute wonder One of the best ways of improving your presentation style is to try presenting to some colleagues, and asking for some direct feedback. If the presentation you're preparing for is a very important one, you should practise anyway, to check your timings, if nothing else.

4 **Body language.** Try not to be too static. It's useful to move around a little, use open body language and hand gestures to emphasize your points. Your body language can involve the audience and keep their interest, whilst showing your enthusiasm for your subject.

5 **Watching the time.** Often, you will be given a time-limit, especially in formal procurement processes. You must try to stick to it. Take off your watch, and lay it down in front of you as a visible sign that you're watching the time.

6 **Handling questions.** By tradition, most presentations conclude with "Any Questions?" Yes, you should leave time at the end for discussion, but I would recommend getting the audience to ask questions during your pitch as well. This way, you can deal with their points in context, and it avoids distractions or the possibility they will forget their questions later.

7 **Buying time.** Of course, you must control the amount of time you spend on dealing with these questions during the presentation. If the issue is a big one, take it 'off-line' and write it up on a sheet of paper as a visible reminder.

It's not just the quality of your offering that's being judged, but you as well.

5.4

Structure your presentation

Let's look at some of the important aspects of presenting, such as structuring your content and delivery for maximum impact. Many of the principles we looked at in relation to writing a proposal have relevance here.

■ **Set the timing.** After you've introduced yourself, it's a good idea to explain to the audience how long you will speak for and/or how many slides you are going to use. This removes any anxiety about what to expect, and allows the audience to relax a little.

■ **Explain your aims.** You might set out an agenda or summary of the main points you wish to cover. This should allow you to explain what your objective is and check this matches the audience's expectations.

■ **Start with the customer.** It is essential that you grab the audience's attention right from the start. Contrary to what you might think, beginning your pitch with 10 PowerPoint slides about how great your company is, and how many customers you have, is the last thing to do. Leave all that until the end, and start by explaining your understanding of their 'pain'. Then demonstrate you understand what their goals are by summarizing the impact of solving that 'pain'.

> "Genius is 1% inspiration and 99% perspiration. Accordingly, a genius is often merely a talented person who has done all of his or her homework"

Thomas Edison, American inventor

■ **Make your solution specific.** Having made your first points directly relevant to the customer's situation, you can now go on and explain how your solution fits those needs.

■ **Tell a story.** If possible, try to describe your proposition in terms of a story the customer can relate to. Use a scenario they will recognize, and try to use examples of how the benefits can be achieved in the context of their own markets. If you have a case study of a similar customer who found success with your solution, this will be powerful in illustrating your story.

■ **Summarize and check understanding.** Throughout your presentation, try to check the audience has got the message you are trying to convey. Finally, you can end with your company overview, and summarize the key strengths of your proposal.

■ **Use a handout.** Provide a brief summary of the content of your presentation in the form of a printed handout: this will make sure that even those who do not take notes will have a permanent reminder of the key benefits and strengths.

Use insights you have gained about the customer's own business problems when planning your presentation.

5.5

Take care with offers and discounts

There is always a strong temptation, when making your initial pitch to a new prospect, to try to strengthen your proposal by offering a special price or discount. Whilst these types of price offers can have their place in effective selling, it is not usually advisable to include them at this stage.

■ **Set expectations.** Your first proposal or presentation to the prospect should preferably include only your standard prices. This is important because it shows that you have confidence that your solution or product is worth it, and that you are not signalling a weak position from the start. There are one or two exceptions to this rule, as we'll see.

case study Recently a lady called me selling advertising space on a website. As soon as she had explained her product, she presented me with an offer of an immediate discount, and rather than asking me some questions or trying to find out if the

■ **Don't lead with a promotion.** Similarly, standard promotions being offered by your company to the general market are not a substitute for first proposing the business value that will justify the price. It's a Marketing job to try to entice new prospects with promotions, but your pitch should be specific and value-based.

■ **You can't sell by negotiating.** Price offers and discounts are really a form of negotiation, and they will have little power if the prospect is not already agreed in principle that they wish to buy. Therefore there is little benefit in trying to persuade or convince a prospect to buy using a price offer upfront. Save the meaningful discounts for the negotiation, not the proposal.

It is acceptable to use a discount or other offer if the prospect is able to offer you something in exchange. A good example of this would be a commitment to purchase by a certain date. If you've discussed this in advance, then you can include it in your proposal. Another scenario where some form of discount may be useful is at the end of a more general pitch to a wider market – such as at a seminar being attended by many prospects from different companies. Here, you could use a special offer combined with a deadline as an incentive.

Price discounts are not a good substitute for a compelling business case based on value.

product might even be of relevance to me, she persisted in offering further discounts. This smacked of desperation, and each time she offered a better price, my perception of the value of her product was eroded.

5.6

Add some sparkle

We have discussed in this chapter the many important aspects of the content of your pitch, whether it is written or presented. However, it is often the emotional reaction of your audience that can make the difference. Let's look at what else you can add to create a pitch that will really stand out.

No matter how well your solution or product fits the needs of the customer – even if you can 'tick every box' – there remains a powerful element of any decision that relates to the credibility and the sense of comfort that the prospect perceives in doing business with you and your company. These are often subjective judgements that the prospect will make about how valuable their relationship with you will be.

■ **'Best practice' advice.** One of the best ways of conveying this message is to give a glimpse of the wider expertise you'll bring if the customer works with you. Here's a simple example: if you're selling a packaged consumer product that sells in small shops, you could enhance your value proposition by offering to include some 'best practice' advice about retail display positioning and marketing of the product, based on the wider experience you and your company possess.

■ **Full backup.** Demonstrate to the prospect that you are backed up by a team, especially if you have people within your business that can act as specialists and advisors. This helps show that you're interested in a partnership, rather than just the sale, and that you'll help the customer get the best from their investment with you.

■ **Personalizing the experience.** Consider whether it is possible for you to cement your credibility by asking an existing customer to take part in your pitch, either by acting as a written reference, or better still, by actually talking to the prospect, perhaps as part of your presentation, about their experiences. There is often no better way to remove any last doubts.

■ **Looking to the future.** Finally, you should look for opportunities to make each prospect feel special. Even the suggestion that you would like to use their experiences with your company as a future case study or 'beacon customer' can have this effect.

Emphasize the added value that a relationship with you and your company can provide.

Gaining commitment

Years ago, when the world of selling and business was perhaps a simpler place, salespeople might have been excused for thinking that selling was all about 'closing' the deal. Now we know it takes a lot more than that to secure long-term business relationships. We must not forget the importance of having a good plan for managing the customer's future business with us.

6.1

Prepare for negotiation

Good preparation, based on an analysis of the facts at your disposal, can make an enormous difference to your ability to negotiate with confidence and from a position of strength.

Even the simplest negotiation is a matter worthy of your careful attention and planning. Here are some of the basics to consider:

■ **Remind yourself of Needs and Wants.** Give some thought not only to your own starting position and desired outcome, but also to those of the customer. In particular, you must remember to prepare for the Needs and Wants of your customer – those things that they must have (mandatory) and those things they would be willing to concede on – their Wants (nice to have).

■ **Know what's valuable.** Both before and during the negotiation, focus on discovering what is of high value to the customer and low cost to you, and what is of high value to you and low cost for them. These are the most tradable types of concessions.

one minute wonder As part of your preparation, you could role-play the negotiation with a colleague, to determine whether you think it will be possible to settle on something that both parties can live with. Remember that obstinacy is the enemy of a good deal. As long as the terms do not fall below your walk-away limit, you should be prepared to make a concession to secure a 'win' for both parties. This isn't a sign of weakness, but of good business practice.

■ **Prioritize concessions.** Now you have a list of things that you might be willing to give away, in exchange for things the buyer might be willing to give. Now put your list into order of priority, with the things you're most willing to concede at the top. This is the order in which you want to trade concessions away.

■ **Be prepared to walk.** You must be willing in principle to walk away if you cannot achieve your minimum terms (your Needs). If you cannot, it means you are desperate and will settle at any cost. You should therefore be clear about what your 'walk-away' limit is – the point at which the deal no longer makes business sense.

■ **Have a fall-back position.** Prepare for the eventuality that you may reach your 'walk-away' limit, by having a clear fall-back position. Usually, in sales, this means having enough other deals in your pipeline so that the loss of this one is not a complete disaster.

Good negotiating technique is all about knowing what to give away and what to ask for.

6.2

Negotiate the deal

Once you have completed your preparation, you're ready to engage in the activity of bargaining, or negotiation. Your aim, if the relationship is important to you, must be to achieve a satisfactory settlement for both you and the buyer. This is called a 'win-win' outcome, and it entails both parties being prepared to make concessions.

Here are key activities that should take place in a professional negotiation:

■ **Set out the agenda.** As a means of setting out the ground-rules, or 'agenda', for the negotiation, sketch out for the buyer the important elements for you in the deal, and ask them to do the same. Really, this means giving each other an overview of your respective Needs and Wants, and acts as an excellent starting point.

■ **Ask open questions.** Throughout the negotiation, use open questions to explore their Needs and Wants. In this way, you can test their assumptions and demands: for example, why is something such as a deadline so important? What will happen if they don't get something they say is mandatory? Use questions to explore the other party's position.

"My father said: "You must never try to make all the money that's in a deal. Let the other fellow make some money too, because if you have a reputation for always making all the money, you won't have many deals**"**

J. Paul Getty, American oil billionaire and philanthropist

■ **Offer conditionally.** You must be willing in a negotiation to make some concessions, based on your preparation, described in 6.1. However, only make a concession in exchange for one from the other party. Whenever you offer to make a concession, do it conditionally, using phrases like "If I do this, will you do that?"

■ **One thing at a time.** You should only offer one concession at a time, not all of them at once! In this way, you might find you agree a deal without having to give away all your concessions. Remember to satisfy the buyer's Needs first, then their Wants.

■ **Hold something back.** Tactically, it is sensible in most negotiations to try to keep at least one concession as a contingency against the inevitable last-minute demand for additional concessions at the point of purchase, especially if there is a competitor involved who may succeed in forcing you to offer one last 'sweetener'.

■ **Write it down.** Make sure you write down the details of the agreement reached straight away, and share this with all parties. This will avoid any misunderstandings later.

Remember that a deal you can live with is better than no deal.

6.3

Price is just one variable

Although most negotiations will involve a range of matters, the question of price will inevitably arise. It may sound like an objection, but remember that prospects who raise the issue of price are indicating a genuine interest in buying, at least in principle. The key here is to remember that price is only one of the variables in the negotiation.

In many ways, price is the easiest matter to deal with: if you have satisfied the prospect on points relating to the value and feasibility of your solution, and price is the only matter remaining, it should be relatively straightforward to find a price both parties can live with.

However, if questions still remain about the value case, or your ability to deliver, these objections must be dealt with before negotiating the price: let's face it, no matter how cheap your product may be, if it won't do the job for the prospect, they will never buy. Therefore, as a general rule, try to deal with price issues last.

■ **Exchanging for something else.** As a principle, you should only reduce your price in exchange for something of equal value to you in the negotiation. Even then, however, it is much better to offer alterna-

❝There is hardly anything in the world that some man can't make a little worse and sell a little cheaper, and the people who consider price only are this man's lawful prey**❞** John Ruskin, English writer, artist and critic

tives in the package, rather than a discount, if you can. This is especially true when the prospect tries to get you to discount by telling you their budget has changed.

■ **Competing with a competitor.** You may be faced with a request to reduce your price based on a competitor's offer. The first step here is to make sure that apples are being compared to apples. Very few solutions or products from two different suppliers are identical. There will be differences, and perhaps these differences will allow you to justify a price higher than your competitor's. The second step is to ask the prospect for evidence of the competitor's price and the components of their offer. If it is genuinely identical to your offer, you can then seek to at least match it. If it isn't, you can examine the reasons why there may be a price difference.

■ **Splitting the difference.** Quite often it is tempting to 'split the difference' between your price and their demand. But consider that if you do this, you are still effectively offering a discount, so try to get something else back in return, even when splitting the difference.

Finally, make sure you're not forced to negotiate a second time, when you'd thought you'd already agreed a price. Check that the price negotiation is the final step in the process.

Always negotiate the price in the context of other variables in your offer.

6.4

Spot the buyer's tactics

It isn't only salespeople who invest time reading books like this one or going on training courses! Buyers do it too, and they might learn specific tactics to try to get the best deal for themselves. Here are four typical tactics employed by buyers:

1 **Hinting at something bigger.** How often have you heard a buyer ask for a big discount now because there's going to be lots of great business in the future? It sounds appealing, and it is if you can get some commitment to some of that extra business. This way, you can increase the size of your deal now, in exchange for better terms. Alternatively, give nothing more away now, but promise to reward the buyer in the future if they continue to buy.

case study Salif was regularly intimidated by a certain buyer who learnt to recognize that during a final negotiation he could be made to offer more and more concessions every time the buyer said something like "I might have to start looking elsewhere..."

2 **Phantom competitor.** If you've created an opportunity, developed a value case with the prospect and have reached the negotiation stage, a favourite tactic of buyers is to invent one or more alternative suppliers offering a better price. Ask who they are and ask for the evidence, such as copy of the quotation. If you don't get satisfactory answers, stick to your deal!

3 **Squashing your enthusiasm.** Experienced buyers may suddenly announce that their budget's smaller than anticipated or that they'll have to look at more suppliers. Rather than immediately caving in to this pressure, recognize this is still a negotiation and suggest 'one last look' before you admit defeat. In this way, show your continued positive outlook and confidence that you can still find an alternative package that will work.

4 **Bad news.** In some cases, the buyer may, at the point where you believe the business is almost won, tell you that you have actually lost. This is a last attempt to scare you into offering more concessions. Point out the time invested by both parties, and indicate your unwillingness to change your offer at such a late stage. Put the pressure back on the buyer to make a decision.

Playing on your fear of failure will only force a concession if you lack confidence in the value of your offer.

Over and over again, the buyer would threaten deadlock, and win another concession. The solution was that the salesperson finally learnt just to say "No" and draw a line. Miraculously, the buyer stopped pushing, realizing he'd pushed too far.

6.5

Handle the competition

The first rule of dealing with the competition is to know as much as possible about your competitors. What are their strengths and weaknesses? If you do your research, you'll be in a stronger position to understand how to compete effectively.

Let's look at four strategies for dealing with the competition.

1 **Nelson's strategy.** Lord Nelson favoured a direct attacking approach if the odds were in his favour. "Never mind manoeuvres, go straight at 'em! You can risk engaging in a direct comparitive fight, and win. Remember, if you're going to knife fight, try to take a gun!" This is sometimes called the Head-to-Head strategy and works when you feel you are in a clearly superior position, for example, if you know you have a better technical solution or other advantage.

2 **Outflank.** This is the strategy to use when you are in second place, competing against a rival who initially holds a superior position. Use your SPEND questioning to try to re-engage, revise the vision of value, and change the decision criteria by exposing more 'pain'.

one minute wonder If you know the strengths and weaknesses of the competition, you can use open questions to seed doubt in the prospect's mind, particularly in areas where you know the competitor has a weakness. Do some comparative analysis, and create a list of these questions.

3 **Delay.** Market leaders do this when faced with a competitor offering a particularly attractive element which they cannot provide. By playing on the customer's anxiety, they will delay a decision until they can make some future commitment to deliver similar functionality. The following strategy is the way to deal with this if you are not the market leader.

4 **Partial retreat.** If you cannot win the whole deal, you can at least try to take some of the business, on the basis that something is better than nothing, and you can develop a strong Number Two position, ready to fight another day. If at least one element of your proposal is favoured by the customer, look for a way of selling just that component, and even committing to work in partnership with the other supplier.

Remember that the most important criteria for deciding between two competitors will often be the quality of the relationship.

Never directly attack the competition, but concentrate on your strengths to expose their weaknesses.

6.6

Ask for the business

When you feel you have reached agreement in your negotiations with your prospect, there will come a time when it is right to ask for their commitment to purchase. If you've followed the techniques so far in this book, you will often find this is a natural and easy thing to do.

You might even find that the customer is by this stage asking you how they can move forward, since you have been successful in creating a compelling vision for your solution. Even so, you will still need to be explicit about asking for their formal decision to proceed.

Here are four different ways of asking for commitment:

1. **Pros and cons.** Take a piece of paper and draw a line down the middle. Say to the customer: "Let's go through the Pros and Cons". Help the customer to list in the Pros column all the benefits of your proposal. Then ask them to list their concerns and worries in the Cons column. But don't help them this time! You'll find the Pros column is usually a lot longer than the

other, and you have a graphic illustration of the weight of the argument for proceeding. Additionally, you have flushed out any 'final objections' and you can start dealing with these individually.

2 **Alternative.** This is helpful for reaching small decisions, such as meeting times, or specifications: simply use the proposition of two or more alternatives to force a positive decision rather than a "No". For example: "Which day would be better for you, Monday 12th or Thursday 15th?" "Can we agree on one pallet or two?"

3 **Assumptive.** Sometimes known as the 'Next Steps' close, this technique uses an assumptive statement as a natural progression from your discussions to invite the prospect to agree to move forward: "Who do we need to liaise with to organize the installation?" or "Who might be the best person for me to work with or to get the contract sent over?" are examples of this technique.

4 **Direct.** There's nothing wrong with simply coming out with a direct request for a decision, or something along the lines of: "Have we done enough to earn your business?" So many salespeople fear asking the direct closing question, because they don't want to provoke a negative response. But if you've covered all the bases, and feel the time is right, why not find out if the prospect is ready to buy?

Always ask clearly for the customer's commitment.

6.7

Overcome the final obstacles

One of the possible outcomes of asking for the business is a negative response. Objections might be raised which may simply be the expression of anxiety or hesitation. In some cases, these 'final objections' really are very serious, because your 'closing' questions may at last have flushed out a major obstacle.

Before you deal with the typical hurdles you might face at this stage, it's important that you try to remember to test-close: this means that you ask the prospect whether, subject to your dealing with their final objections satisfactorily, they will be happy then to proceed. This is the best way to prevent even more objections being thrown at you.

■ **Customer wants to think about it.** This is the classic 'hesitation' objection. You can of course respond by asking what the prospect needs to think about, and that way, expose their real worry. Alternatively, this is a good moment to use the Pros and Cons close we looked at in the previous chapter. If the prospect persists with this objection it may be an indication that they are simply unable to make a decision, or lack the authority.

> "Remember, a real decision is measured by the fact that you've taken new action. If there's no action, you haven't truly decided" **Anthony Robbins, American motivational writer**

■ **Customer wants to consult.** Sometimes, the prospect will tell you they need to talk to their colleagues before they can go ahead. This may be another indication that they do indeed require a higher authority to take the decision for them after all. Find out who they want to consult. It may be that you will discover a new buyer introduced at the last minute, such as a procurement officer. The danger here is that the negotiation phase is re-opened. If you believe you have agreed terms already, hold your ground and ask to speak directly to the new buyer involved.

■ **Customer develops 'spendophobia'.** This is what I call that sense of panic that some buyers can feel at the moment of making a significant purchase – and often for a short while afterwards. Feelings of anxiety, doubt and insecurity can combine to create an emotional hurdle that has sometimes, in my experience, led a customer to abandon the deal, at least while they go back and review their decision. If a competitor can exploit this phenomenon, you can lose the deal altogether! The answer is to 'hand-hold' the customer throughout, reassuring them that you will not let them down, and re-emphasizing the benefits of their decision.

Be ready to deal with those last-minute dangers created by the buyer's sense of personal risk.

6.8

Know when to retreat

It's worth spending a little time looking at the unpleasant possibility that you may eventually lose the deal, the typical reasons for this, and what options you may have to rescue something positive from the experience.

■ **When you choose to walk away.** Firstly, it is worth noting that you may on some occasions choose to lose a deal for rational reasons. This might sound crazy, but an assessment of the cost to you, in effort, time and resources, of this sale, versus the loss of opportunity elsewhere, may make a good case for walking away.

■ **The 'no-win' scenario.** Just as significant is the role that the buyers' personalities and behaviours play. It is not uncommon to end up in a 'no-win' position with a prospect who is impossible to deal with reasonably, because they insist on bluffing or lying to you. They promised you

one minute wonder It is a good exercise periodically to review your losses, and with the benefit of hindsight, develop some improvements in your approach. There's a lot you can learn about your own selling tactics and the ways you can position your offerings in the future by treating defeat as a lesson.

"Failure is simply the opportunity to begin again, this time more intelligently" **Henry Ford**

they could and would buy, but never actually did anything about it. Maybe some people just enjoy the attention salespeople give them.

■ **When the prospect refuses to make a concession.** Equally, some people never want to back down or make a concession. I call this 'wrestling with a pig'. You're unlikely to win, and you get covered in mud trying to! In these situations, it is much better to recognize what you're dealing with, and stop wasting your time.

■ **The final offer.** Assuming, however, that you have lost out in a fair fight, you should at least try to retreat with dignity and look at options for making the competitor's life more difficult in the process. You might take advantage of their 'spendophobia' to put a final, heavily discounted offer on the table: you are still unlikely to change the decision, but you will create serious pressure for the competitor; you might suggest they split their risk, and take on a second supplier as well. What additional enhancements or components could you still offer?

■ **Thinking of the future.** You also have the added option of maintaining a good relationship with the customer for the future: promise to stay in contact to review their progress, offer to become their 'back-up' option should the chosen supplier let them down, and at all times, stay polite and calm, explaining that although on this occasion you weren't successful you'll expect to be able to offer your services the next time they have a requirement.

Live to fight another day by showing good grace.

6.9

Know what to do after you've sold

Let's take a look at some of the behaviours you should practise once you've been successful and landed the deal. You might think there's nothing much left to do but to go out and celebrate, but you've still got some work to do!

■ **Shut up!** As we noted in 4.9, immediately after asking for the business, keep control of your mouth and try not to say very much until the signature is on the contract!

■ **Get it in writing.** A verbal decision to buy is helpful, but not the whole story. Perhaps that competitor is still waiting in the wings to upset your plans? Any manner of new worries or objections might occur to the prospect afterwards. Therefore, always get something in writing there and then, even if it just an email at this stage.

■ **Say thank you.** Don't forget to say thank you for the trust the buyer has put in you and your company. Remind the customer that you intend to make every effort to make sure you won't let them down. This is part of that 'hand-holding' exercise we discussed previously, apart from being simple good manners.

"We see our customers as invited guests to a party, and we are the hosts" Jeff Bezos, Founder, Amazon.com

■ **Check delivery and payment.** Once you have written confirmation of the purchase in your hands, take personal care to make sure that delivery happens as promised. Remember, the invoice won't get paid until you deliver, and you haven't really sold until you've collected the cash!

■ **Stay engaged.** Too many salespeople tend to hand over the fulfilment of an order to colleagues, so they can concentrate on new sales, but if you stay in touch throughout the delivery process, you'll reap the benefits, not least the respect of the customer.

■ **Create the next sale.** We'll look at managing existing customers in more detail later, but in the immediate aftermath of making a sale, you can start setting up the conditions for the next one. Use your new customer's commitment and interest in you to build some new contacts particularly at more senior levels, and publicize your success elsewhere within the customer's organization.

■ **Referrals.** One of the most effective ways of finding new business leads is to ask a new customer whom they would approach if they woke up tomorrow morning and found they were doing your job. Ask them for at least one name in their business network who might be interested in what you can offer.

Remember that a sale is just one transaction, but your business is based on continuing relationships.

6.10

Manage your customer

Selling, of course, is not just about closing a series of deals. Successful salespeople these days must be effective relationship managers, business advisors and problem solvers. This means putting in some effort with the customer, even when there is no specific deal on the table. It means having a long-term plan.

■ **Make a plan.** You may capture customer details in a computer system and keep records of your activities in all manner of formats, but you should also create an account plan which describes your objectives, strategy and tactics. It should include some analysis of what you know about new opportunities, and what you will do to discover new information that will help you to develop the relationship further.

case study A few years ago, I worked as Sales Director for a company that sold valuable data products which required an annual license payment. The problem was that one or two salespeople came to rely on the revenue and got complacent, only

■ **Work out a strategy.** Your customer development plan needs to be based on a sensible objective for the whole account. Your strategy can be as simple as a few high-level statements of intent. In any case, you should try to formulate a strategy made up of small achievable steps which will involve your working closely with the customer and learning more about their business.

■ **What don't you know?** One of the most important aspects of a good account plan is its ability to show you what you don't know. Your first sale may only have revealed a small part of the way the customer's business works. For example, try drawing out the detailed organization chart for the whole customer enterprise. Any gaps in your knowledge need to be turned into sales actions.

■ **White space.** In larger accounts, you can undertake some analysis of the overall potential by relating your range of solutions or products to the various functions or departments of their business. Where have you already sold? Where else could you replicate that success, or offer another product or solution. You can map this out on a single sheet of paper, and reveal the 'white space' in the account.

■ **Stay engaged.** It goes without saying that the effort required to sell to an existing customer will be much less than a new prospect. However, if you ignore your existing customers because you are spending too much time prospecting, they will quite quickly lose sight of you and become just as hard to sell to as a new prospect.

Your existing customers are a precious asset: treat them accordingly.

remembering to call the customer a few weeks before the renewal payment was due each year. It was quite a shock when one of the largest of these companies revealed they had been researching the market and had found an alternative supplier.

The right attitude

I firmly believe, based on the observation of consistently successful salespeople over many years, that the single most important element about top performers is their attitude – something which cannot necessarily be learnt, but must come from within. Developing the right attitude will make all the difference, because successful selling, unlike many other professions, relies on your personal behaviour.

7.1

Prepare and persist

Although, as I mentioned in the introduction to this chapter, attitude is so important, the other two key components of success in selling are knowledge and skills. Both of these can be improved with training, practice and a bit of self-analysis.

If you are serious about becoming a consistently successful sales-person, then you must start to think and act like a professional. Selling is a serious profession. In fact, the most useful comparison to make is with professional sports people who, like us, need to combine their skills with knowledge and personal motivation to win.

Golfers or tennis players, even those at the very top of their professional game, never avoid practising every day and trying to

one minute wonder Each week, set yourself a personal development goal, based on one new skill in this book. Then tell your manager what you want to practise, and ask them to give you the benefit of their experience and feedback. At the end of the week, review honestly together how you could have done it better.

"You will either step forward into growth or you will step back into safety" Abraham Maslow, American psychologist

improve. They develop their self-confidence through a process of incremental improvement, based on a careful analysis of their faults and weaknesses.

■ **Find a mentor.** Some people are good at observing where they go wrong. Most of us however, need the frank and constructive feedback of a good coach or mentor. Try to find someone within your business, perhaps your manager, who is willing to observe you in action, and provide some critique of your performance.

■ **Keep learning.** In this way, every interaction you have with a customer can become an opportunity to practise a new skill, or learn something new about your markets, your products and yourself. Every failure can be an opportunity to assess what went wrong, and try something different next time.

■ **Stay focused.** Coupled with an interest in practise, persistence in the face of rejection is a fundamental attribute found in great salespeople. The ability to develop some mental toughness and a focus on trying again and again until you get it right is vital, and this is driven by an understanding that even when everything is going against you, blaming others is not the answer.

Persistence is not the same as obstinacy: obstinate people don't think they need to change.

7.2

Define your success

Developing the right attitude for success in sales is really about accepting responsibility for your own results and finding ways to motivate yourself. It's the difference between thinking "I have to do this" (to keep my job, or to please my boss) and "I want to do this" (to achieve my own goals).

■ **Build a vision of success.** Self-motivation, and therefore determination and persistence, come from having a set of personal goals in which you genuinely believe, and which you are willing to make sacrifices to achieve. But goals on their own don't really mean very much unless you can also clearly visualize the effect on you, personally, if you achieve them. So the starting point is actually to create a vision of success

case study I have a friend who recently inherited an old, very dilapidated house which he decided to renovate himself. It was going to be a huge task which would require an awful lot of hard work and dedication from him. I wondered how he would keep himself motivated through the long weeks to come. "Before I start on each room, I think

"Winning is everything"

Damon Hill, English racing driver

in your own mind and focus on that. Ask yourself: what will success feel like? How much better will my life be (and why)?

You may have obvious business goals set for you by your organization or business, expressed in terms of sales value, for example. You must try to translate these into something exciting and meaningful for you personally, if you achieve them. If you have a business goal that results in increased earnings through commission payments, visualize what you will be able to do in the future with that additional income.

■ **Personalize your vision.** For many salespeople, this often means the chance to acquire material possessions, enjoy a better standard of living, educate their children or just treat themselves. But I have met many great salespeople who were motivated by less quantifiable things, such as the status and recognition that comes with success, or the chance to turn a dream of setting up their own business into reality.

If you can create a personal vision of what success will mean for you, and then keep this in clear focus each day, you will find that your determination to strive under pressure will not falter.

Turn your everyday business goals into visions of success.

about how great I'm going to feel walking through it when it is finally repainted, with new floors and fittings. I keep that vision in my mind while I'm working." He did the same thing for the whole project, reminding himself of the personal satisfaction he would derive from finally being able to move in and live there.

7.3

Manage yourself

You have only a limited amount of time each week to do all of the things we've covered in this book. You can't do all of them all of the time, and some are clearly more important than others, or will require more attention, depending on the goals you have set. Here are some tips to help you get organized.

■ **Prioritize tasks.** Firstly, write down every selling activity that you need to do each week, such as new business telephone prospecting, customer planning, sales visits, writing proposals and so on.

■ **Schedule tasks.** You should now schedule these tasks in your diary, putting the most important first. This process is a bit like trying to fill a bucket with a combination of large rocks, small stones and gravel: if you put the gravel in first, then the small rocks, you'll find no room left for the large rocks. If you do it the other way around, you'll find the gravel, which now goes in last, fits neatly around the larger rocks!

■ **Scrutinize time.** If you're wondering which are the 'large rocks' – or most important tasks you should schedule first, ask yourself which tasks represent actual, real selling to prospects or customers. This is your active

one minute wonder Keep a list of the regular sales activities you do each week, and then note down the amount of time you spend on these and the amount you spend on dead, or passive time when you are not actually selling. Now put each of the priority sales tasks into your weekly diary, and try replacing at least half of the dead time with new selling tasks.

selling time, when you are face to face, or talking with a customer. All other time, to be honest, is dead time, or at least passive time. You need to maximize your active selling time and prioritize those tasks.

■ **Single focus or multiple tasks?** You'll probably by this stage have found you have far too much to get done, but don't panic! You might be tempted to try doing 15 different things at once. Actually, most behavioural research has shown that concentrating entirely on one task at a time is much more effective than multi-tasking.

■ **Distractions.** The environment in which you work will make a lot of difference to your overall effectiveness. Perhaps a busy, noisy office helps to motivate you. Perhaps you do need some peace and quiet for certain tasks though. Work out some options for different sales activities, and don't be afraid to tell colleagues you don't want to be disturbed on occasions.

Be ruthless about prioritizing your active selling time.

7.4

Develop your creativity, enthusiasm and drive

Here are three more attributes of great salespeople that, like attitude, can't be taught, but can be developed and improved by you, if you want to succeed badly enough. They're not essential qualities, but they do set the top performer apart from the rest.

1 **Creativity.** How good are you at innovating and coming up with new ideas? Sales offers us countless opportunities to think up new ways of dealing with a market, a prospect or a business problem, and often, we're required to 'think on our feet', especially in negotiations or consultation with customers. I'm not asking you to become an inventor of new solutions, but I am suggesting that you develop an entrepreneurial and positive approach, with the courage to suggest or attempt alternatives that could give you an advantage in a sale.

2 **Enthusiasm.** Not only is enthusiasm infectious, but in fact it can make the difference in helping a customer to decide! A flat, uninterested attitude, displayed in a bored and tired voice, will send any buyer with a choice away to your competitors. Enthu-

> **"**Go as far as you can see; when you get there, you'll be able to see farther**"** **JP Morgan, American banker**

siasm is simply the outward display of the right attitude – customers will notice this, and respond positively. It helps if you truly believe in your product or service, but even if you don't, your enthusiasm is a sign that you believe in yourself!

3 **Drive.** If I were to ask you whether you thought you could swim across the 26 miles of the English Channel, would you even bother considering how you would do it, before telling me you couldn't? What if I then told you I would pay you a million pounds if you did it? You might start thinking about a possible training regime, and begin to imagine yourself out there, swimming for six hours. What's changed? Not your ability or your knowledge of how hard it would be, but your desire to succeed because of the incentive.

Think about your current business goals and ask yourself just how important their achievement is to you. If the answer is "Not that important," you haven't got big enough goals!

Your success depends on combining your skills and knowledge with an enthusiastic, inspiring attitude.

Jargon buster

Buying signal

Comment from a prospect that indicates he or she is visualizing buying your product or service. The most common buying signal is the question: "How much is it?" Others are questions or comments like: "What's the lead-time?", "Who else do you supply?"

Canvass

The process of researching a customer or market, usually by telephone to determine their interest or gather information.

Closing

The act of gaining final commitment to purchase from a customer.

Closed question

A question that prompts a yes or no answer, or another short answer with just two possible options.

Cold calling

The first telephone call made to a prospective customer. Cold calling is also known as canvassing, telephone canvassing, prospecting, telephone prospecting.

Concession

Used in the context of negotiating, an aspect of the sale which has a real or perceived value, that is given away or conceded by the seller (more usually) or the buyer.

Deal

Common business parlance for a sale or purchase, or an agreement or arrangement. It is a colloquial term so avoid using it in serious company as it can sound flippant.

FAB

Features, Advantages & Benefits – the links between a product description, its advantage over others, and the gain derived by the customer from using it. One of the central techniques used in the presentation stage of the selling process.

Objection

A point of resistance raised by a prospect, usually price ("It's too expensive.").

Open question

A question that gains information, usually beginning with who, what, why, where, when, how, or more subtly "tell me about".

Package

In a selling context this is another term for the product offer; it's the whole product and service offering at a given price, upon given terms.

Pipeline

The pipeline is the total number of business opportunities the salesperson is working on. Opportunities need to be fed into the pipeline to drop out the other end as sales.

Proposal/sales proposal

Usually a written offer with specification, prices, outline terms and conditions, and warranty arrangements.

Prospect

A prospective customer.

Referral

A recommendation or personal introduction.

Research/research call

The act of gathering information about a market or customer, that will help progress or enable a sales approach.

Sales cycle/selling cycle

The time and process between first contact with the customer to when the sale is made.

Sales report

A business report of sales results, activities, trends, etc., traditionally completed by a sales manager, but increasingly now the responsibility of sales people too.

Sector/market sector

A part of the market that can be categorized and then targeted according to its own criteria and characteristics; sectors are often described as 'vertical', meaning an industry type, or 'horizontal', meaning a grouping that spans a number of vertical sectors, e.g. geographical, defined by age, or size etc.

Target/sales target

The issued (or ideally agreed) level of sales performance for a sales person or team over a given period. Bonus payments, sales commissions, etc. can depend on targets.

Telemarketing

Any pre-sales activity conducted by telephone, usually by specially trained telemarketing personnel – for instance, research, appointment-making, product promotion.

Telesales

Selling by telephone contact alone; used typically for low order values of a recognizable product or service.

Territory

The geographical area of responsibility of a sales person or a team or a sales organization

USP

Unique selling point or proposition – this is what makes the product offer competitively strong and without direct comparison; generally the most valuable unique advantage of a product or service, for the market or prospect in question.

Variable

Aspect of the sale that can be changed in order to better meet the needs of the seller and/or the buyer. Typical variables are price, quantity, lead-time, payment terms, technical factors, styling factors, spare parts, back-up and breakdown service, routine maintenance, installation, warranty.

Further reading

Blanchard, Kenneth and Mackay, Harvey *Swim With Sharks Without Being Eaten Alive* (Sphere, 1989) ISBN 978-0751507034

Blythe, Jim *Sales and Sales Management* (Blackhall, 2000) ISBN 1-842180-10-X

Caan, James *The Real Deal* (Virgin, 2009) ISBN 978-0753515099

Carnegie, Dale *How to Win Friends and Influence People* (Vermillion, 2007) ISBN 978-0091906818

Covey, Stephen R. *7 Habits of Highly Effective People: Powerful Lessons in Personal Change* (Simon and Schuster, 2004) ISBN 978-0743272452

Eades, Keith *The New Solution Selling* (McGraw Hill, 2004) ISBN 0-07-1435395

Etherington, Bob *Cold Calling for Chickens* (Cyan Books and Marshall Cavendish, 2006) ISBN 978-1904879817

Fielder, Robin *Outsell Your Competition* (McGraw Hill, 2002) ISBN 0-07-7099370

Fisher, Roger, Ury, William and Patton, Bruce *Getting to Yes* (Random House, 2003) ISBN 978-1844131464

Gitomer, Jeffrey *The Sales Bible* (John Wiley, 2003) ISBN 978-0471456292

Kennedy, Gavin *Everything is Negotiable* (Random House, 2008) ISBN 978-1847940018

McCormack, Mark H. *Never Wrestle with a Pig* (Penguin Putnam, 2002) ISBN: 978-0141002088

McCormack, Mark H. *What You'll Never Learn on the Internet* (Harper Collins Business, 2000) ISBN 978-0-0025-7171-5

McCormack, Mark H. *What They Don't Teach You at Harvard Business School* (Profile Business, 1994) ISBN 978-1861975645

Schiffman, Stephen *Cold Calling Techniques* (Adams Media, 1987) ISBN: 10-1-59869-148-1

Tracy, Brian *Advanced Selling Strategies* (Simon & Schuster, 1996) ISBN 978-0684824741

Washburn, Harry *Why People Don't Buy Things* (Perseus, 1999) ISBN 978-0738201573

Useful websites

www.redlineassociates.co.uk – professional Sales Training & Coaching; Sales Performance Improvement programmes.

www.coldcallingpodcast.com

www.modernselling.com

www.linkedin.com – LinkedIn Business Networking

www.jigsaw.com – Jigsaw Business Directory

www.businessballs.com/salestraining.htm – Businessballs sales techniques

www.BusinessSecrets.net

WITHDRAWN FROM STOCK